© Copyright 2021 - All rights reserved.

You may not reproduce, duplicate or send the contents of this book without direct written permission from the author. You cannot hereby despite any circumstance blame the publisher or hold him or her to legal responsibility for any reparation, compensations, or monetary forfeiture owing to the information included herein, either in a direct or an indirect way.

Legal Notice: This book has copyright protection. You can use the book for personal purpose. You should not sell, use, alter, distribute, quote, take excerpts or paraphrase in part or whole the material contained in this book without obtaining the permission of the author first.

Disclaimer Notice: You must take note that the information in this document is for casual reading and entertainment purposes only.
We have made every attempt to provide accurate, up to date and reliable information. We do not express or imply guarantees of any kind. The persons who read admit that the writer is not occupied in giving legal, financial, medical or other advice. We put this book content by sourcing various places.

Please consult a licensed professional before you try any techniques shown in this book. By going through this document, the book lover comes to an agreement that under no situation is the author accountable for any forfeiture, direct or indirect, which they may incur because of the use of material contained in this document, including, but not limited to, errors, omissions, or inaccuracies.

Food Log

This book belongs to:
_____

By Cucu Suru

Date _____

Breakfast

Time	Items	Serving	Cals	Sugar	Protein	Fiber	Carbs	Fat

Lunch

Time	Items	Serving	Cals	Sugar	Protein	Fiber	Carbs	Fat

Dinner

Time	Items	Serving	Cals	Sugar	Protein	Fiber	Carbs	Fat

Snacks

Time	Items	Serving	Cals	Sugar	Protein	Fiber	Carbs	Fat

Total

Serving	Cals	Sugar	Protein	Fiber	Carbs	Fat

Date _____

Breakfast

Time	Items	Serving	Cals	Sugar	Protein	Fiber	Carbs	Fat

Lunch

Time	Items	Serving	Cals	Sugar	Protein	Fiber	Carbs	Fat

Dinner

Time	Items	Serving	Cals	Sugar	Protein	Fiber	Carbs	Fat

Snacks

Time	Items	Serving	Cals	Sugar	Protein	Fiber	Carbs	Fat

Total

Serving	Cals	Sugar	Protein	Fiber	Carbs	Fat

Date _____

Breakfast

Time	Items	Serving	Cals	Sugar	Protein	Fiber	Carbs	Fat

Lunch

Time	Items	Serving	Cals	Sugar	Protein	Fiber	Carbs	Fat

Dinner

Time	Items	Serving	Cals	Sugar	Protein	Fiber	Carbs	Fat

Snacks

Time	Items	Serving	Cals	Sugar	Protein	Fiber	Carbs	Fat

Total

Serving	Cals	Sugar	Protein	Fiber	Carbs	Fat

Date _____

Breakfast

Time	Items	Serving	Cals	Sugar	Protein	Fiber	Carbs	Fat

Lunch

Time	Items	Serving	Cals	Sugar	Protein	Fiber	Carbs	Fat

Dinner

Time	Items	Serving	Cals	Sugar	Protein	Fiber	Carbs	Fat

Snacks

Time	Items	Serving	Cals	Sugar	Protein	Fiber	Carbs	Fat

Total

Serving	Cals	Sugar	Protein	Fiber	Carbs	Fat

Date _____

Breakfast

Time	Items	Serving	Cals	Sugar	Protein	Fiber	Carbs	Fat

Lunch

Time	Items	Serving	Cals	Sugar	Protein	Fiber	Carbs	Fat

Dinner

Time	Items	Serving	Cals	Sugar	Protein	Fiber	Carbs	Fat

Snacks

Time	Items	Serving	Cals	Sugar	Protein	Fiber	Carbs	Fat

Total

Serving	Cals	Sugar	Protein	Fiber	Carbs	Fat

Date _____

Breakfast

Time	Items	Serving	Cals	Sugar	Protein	Fiber	Carbs	Fat

Lunch

Time	Items	Serving	Cals	Sugar	Protein	Fiber	Carbs	Fat

Dinner

Time	Items	Serving	Cals	Sugar	Protein	Fiber	Carbs	Fat

Snacks

Time	Items	Serving	Cals	Sugar	Protein	Fiber	Carbs	Fat

Total

Serving	Cals	Sugar	Protein	Fiber	Carbs	Fat

Date _____

Breakfast

Time	Items	Serving	Cals	Sugar	Protein	Fiber	Carbs	Fat

Lunch

Time	Items	Serving	Cals	Sugar	Protein	Fiber	Carbs	Fat

Dinner

Time	Items	Serving	Cals	Sugar	Protein	Fiber	Carbs	Fat

Snacks

Time	Items	Serving	Cals	Sugar	Protein	Fiber	Carbs	Fat

Total

Serving	Cals	Sugar	Protein	Fiber	Carbs	Fat

Date _____

Breakfast

Time	Items	Serving	Cals	Sugar	Protein	Fiber	Carbs	Fat

Lunch

Time	Items	Serving	Cals	Sugar	Protein	Fiber	Carbs	Fat

Dinner

Time	Items	Serving	Cals	Sugar	Protein	Fiber	Carbs	Fat

Snacks

Time	Items	Serving	Cals	Sugar	Protein	Fiber	Carbs	Fat

Total

Serving	Cals	Sugar	Protein	Fiber	Carbs	Fat

Date _____

Breakfast

Time	Items	Serving	Cals	Sugar	Protein	Fiber	Carbs	Fat

Lunch

Time	Items	Serving	Cals	Sugar	Protein	Fiber	Carbs	Fat

Dinner

Time	Items	Serving	Cals	Sugar	Protein	Fiber	Carbs	Fat

Snacks

Time	Items	Serving	Cals	Sugar	Protein	Fiber	Carbs	Fat

Total

Serving	Cals	Sugar	Protein	Fiber	Carbs	Fat

Date _____

Breakfast

Time	Items	Serving	Cals	Sugar	Protein	Fiber	Carbs	Fat

Lunch

Time	Items	Serving	Cals	Sugar	Protein	Fiber	Carbs	Fat

Dinner

Time	Items	Serving	Cals	Sugar	Protein	Fiber	Carbs	Fat

Snacks

Time	Items	Serving	Cals	Sugar	Protein	Fiber	Carbs	Fat

Total

Serving	Cals	Sugar	Protein	Fiber	Carbs	Fat

Date _____

Breakfast

Time	Items	Serving	Cals	Sugar	Protein	Fiber	Carbs	Fat

Lunch

Time	Items	Serving	Cals	Sugar	Protein	Fiber	Carbs	Fat

Dinner

Time	Items	Serving	Cals	Sugar	Protein	Fiber	Carbs	Fat

Snacks

Time	Items	Serving	Cals	Sugar	Protein	Fiber	Carbs	Fat

Total

Serving	Cals	Sugar	Protein	Fiber	Carbs	Fat

Date _____

Breakfast

Time	Items	Serving	Cals	Sugar	Protein	Fiber	Carbs	Fat

Lunch

Time	Items	Serving	Cals	Sugar	Protein	Fiber	Carbs	Fat

Dinner

Time	Items	Serving	Cals	Sugar	Protein	Fiber	Carbs	Fat

Snacks

Time	Items	Serving	Cals	Sugar	Protein	Fiber	Carbs	Fat

Total

Serving	Cals	Sugar	Protein	Fiber	Carbs	Fat

Date _____

Breakfast

Time	Items	Serving	Cals	Sugar	Protein	Fiber	Carbs	Fat

Lunch

Time	Items	Serving	Cals	Sugar	Protein	Fiber	Carbs	Fat

Dinner

Time	Items	Serving	Cals	Sugar	Protein	Fiber	Carbs	Fat

Snacks

Time	Items	Serving	Cals	Sugar	Protein	Fiber	Carbs	Fat

Total

Serving	Cals	Sugar	Protein	Fiber	Carbs	Fat

Date _____

Breakfast

Time	Items	Serving	Cals	Sugar	Protein	Fiber	Carbs	Fat

Lunch

Time	Items	Serving	Cals	Sugar	Protein	Fiber	Carbs	Fat

Dinner

Time	Items	Serving	Cals	Sugar	Protein	Fiber	Carbs	Fat

Snacks

Time	Items	Serving	Cals	Sugar	Protein	Fiber	Carbs	Fat

Total

Serving	Cals	Sugar	Protein	Fiber	Carbs	Fat

Date _____

Breakfast

Time	Items	Serving	Cals	Sugar	Protein	Fiber	Carbs	Fat

Lunch

Time	Items	Serving	Cals	Sugar	Protein	Fiber	Carbs	Fat

Dinner

Time	Items	Serving	Cals	Sugar	Protein	Fiber	Carbs	Fat

Snacks

Time	Items	Serving	Cals	Sugar	Protein	Fiber	Carbs	Fat

Total

Serving	Cals	Sugar	Protein	Fiber	Carbs	Fat

Date _____

Breakfast

Time	Items	Serving	Cals	Sugar	Protein	Fiber	Carbs	Fat

Lunch

Time	Items	Serving	Cals	Sugar	Protein	Fiber	Carbs	Fat

Dinner

Time	Items	Serving	Cals	Sugar	Protein	Fiber	Carbs	Fat

Snacks

Time	Items	Serving	Cals	Sugar	Protein	Fiber	Carbs	Fat

Total

Serving	Cals	Sugar	Protein	Fiber	Carbs	Fat

Date _____

Breakfast

Time	Items	Serving	Cals	Sugar	Protein	Fiber	Carbs	Fat

Lunch

Time	Items	Serving	Cals	Sugar	Protein	Fiber	Carbs	Fat

Dinner

Time	Items	Serving	Cals	Sugar	Protein	Fiber	Carbs	Fat

Snacks

Time	Items	Serving	Cals	Sugar	Protein	Fiber	Carbs	Fat

Total

Serving	Cals	Sugar	Protein	Fiber	Carbs	Fat

Date _____

Breakfast

Time	Items	Serving	Cals	Sugar	Protein	Fiber	Carbs	Fat

Lunch

Time	Items	Serving	Cals	Sugar	Protein	Fiber	Carbs	Fat

Dinner

Time	Items	Serving	Cals	Sugar	Protein	Fiber	Carbs	Fat

Snacks

Time	Items	Serving	Cals	Sugar	Protein	Fiber	Carbs	Fat

Total

Serving	Cals	Sugar	Protein	Fiber	Carbs	Fat

Date _____

Breakfast

Time	Items	Serving	Cals	Sugar	Protein	Fiber	Carbs	Fat

Lunch

Time	Items	Serving	Cals	Sugar	Protein	Fiber	Carbs	Fat

Dinner

Time	Items	Serving	Cals	Sugar	Protein	Fiber	Carbs	Fat

Snacks

Time	Items	Serving	Cals	Sugar	Protein	Fiber	Carbs	Fat

Total

Serving	Cals	Sugar	Protein	Fiber	Carbs	Fat

Date _____

Breakfast

Time	Items	Serving	Cals	Sugar	Protein	Fiber	Carbs	Fat

Lunch

Time	Items	Serving	Cals	Sugar	Protein	Fiber	Carbs	Fat

Dinner

Time	Items	Serving	Cals	Sugar	Protein	Fiber	Carbs	Fat

Snacks

Time	Items	Serving	Cals	Sugar	Protein	Fiber	Carbs	Fat

Total

Serving	Cals	Sugar	Protein	Fiber	Carbs	Fat

Date _____

Breakfast

Time	Items	Serving	Cals	Sugar	Protein	Fiber	Carbs	Fat

Lunch

Time	Items	Serving	Cals	Sugar	Protein	Fiber	Carbs	Fat

Dinner

Time	Items	Serving	Cals	Sugar	Protein	Fiber	Carbs	Fat

Snacks

Time	Items	Serving	Cals	Sugar	Protein	Fiber	Carbs	Fat

Total

Serving	Cals	Sugar	Protein	Fiber	Carbs	Fat

Date _____

Breakfast

Time	Items	Serving	Cals	Sugar	Protein	Fiber	Carbs	Fat

Lunch

Time	Items	Serving	Cals	Sugar	Protein	Fiber	Carbs	Fat

Dinner

Time	Items	Serving	Cals	Sugar	Protein	Fiber	Carbs	Fat

Snacks

Time	Items	Serving	Cals	Sugar	Protein	Fiber	Carbs	Fat

Total

Serving	Cals	Sugar	Protein	Fiber	Carbs	Fat

Date _____

Breakfast

Time	Items	Serving	Cals	Sugar	Protein	Fiber	Carbs	Fat

Lunch

Time	Items	Serving	Cals	Sugar	Protein	Fiber	Carbs	Fat

Dinner

Time	Items	Serving	Cals	Sugar	Protein	Fiber	Carbs	Fat

Snacks

Time	Items	Serving	Cals	Sugar	Protein	Fiber	Carbs	Fat

Total

Serving	Cals	Sugar	Protein	Fiber	Carbs	Fat

Date _____

Breakfast

Time	Items	Serving	Cals	Sugar	Protein	Fiber	Carbs	Fat

Lunch

Time	Items	Serving	Cals	Sugar	Protein	Fiber	Carbs	Fat

Dinner

Time	Items	Serving	Cals	Sugar	Protein	Fiber	Carbs	Fat

Snacks

Time	Items	Serving	Cals	Sugar	Protein	Fiber	Carbs	Fat

Total

Serving	Cals	Sugar	Protein	Fiber	Carbs	Fat

Date _____

Breakfast

Time	Items	Serving	Cals	Sugar	Protein	Fiber	Carbs	Fat

Lunch

Time	Items	Serving	Cals	Sugar	Protein	Fiber	Carbs	Fat

Dinner

Time	Items	Serving	Cals	Sugar	Protein	Fiber	Carbs	Fat

Snacks

Time	Items	Serving	Cals	Sugar	Protein	Fiber	Carbs	Fat

Total

Serving	Cals	Sugar	Protein	Fiber	Carbs	Fat

Date _____

Breakfast

Time	Items	Serving	Cals	Sugar	Protein	Fiber	Carbs	Fat

Lunch

Time	Items	Serving	Cals	Sugar	Protein	Fiber	Carbs	Fat

Dinner

Time	Items	Serving	Cals	Sugar	Protein	Fiber	Carbs	Fat

Snacks

Time	Items	Serving	Cals	Sugar	Protein	Fiber	Carbs	Fat

Total

Serving	Cals	Sugar	Protein	Fiber	Carbs	Fat

Date _____

Breakfast

Time	Items	Serving	Cals	Sugar	Protein	Fiber	Carbs	Fat

Lunch

Time	Items	Serving	Cals	Sugar	Protein	Fiber	Carbs	Fat

Dinner

Time	Items	Serving	Cals	Sugar	Protein	Fiber	Carbs	Fat

Snacks

Time	Items	Serving	Cals	Sugar	Protein	Fiber	Carbs	Fat

Total

Serving	Cals	Sugar	Protein	Fiber	Carbs	Fat

Date _____

Breakfast

Time	Items	Serving	Cals	Sugar	Protein	Fiber	Carbs	Fat

Lunch

Time	Items	Serving	Cals	Sugar	Protein	Fiber	Carbs	Fat

Dinner

Time	Items	Serving	Cals	Sugar	Protein	Fiber	Carbs	Fat

Snacks

Time	Items	Serving	Cals	Sugar	Protein	Fiber	Carbs	Fat

Total

Serving	Cals	Sugar	Protein	Fiber	Carbs	Fat

Date _____

Breakfast

Time	Items	Serving	Cals	Sugar	Protein	Fiber	Carbs	Fat

Lunch

Time	Items	Serving	Cals	Sugar	Protein	Fiber	Carbs	Fat

Dinner

Time	Items	Serving	Cals	Sugar	Protein	Fiber	Carbs	Fat

Snacks

Time	Items	Serving	Cals	Sugar	Protein	Fiber	Carbs	Fat

Total

Serving	Cals	Sugar	Protein	Fiber	Carbs	Fat

Date _____

Breakfast

Time	Items	Serving	Cals	Sugar	Protein	Fiber	Carbs	Fat

Lunch

Time	Items	Serving	Cals	Sugar	Protein	Fiber	Carbs	Fat

Dinner

Time	Items	Serving	Cals	Sugar	Protein	Fiber	Carbs	Fat

Snacks

Time	Items	Serving	Cals	Sugar	Protein	Fiber	Carbs	Fat

Total

Serving	Cals	Sugar	Protein	Fiber	Carbs	Fat

Date _____

Breakfast

Time	Items	Serving	Cals	Sugar	Protein	Fiber	Carbs	Fat

Lunch

Time	Items	Serving	Cals	Sugar	Protein	Fiber	Carbs	Fat

Dinner

Time	Items	Serving	Cals	Sugar	Protein	Fiber	Carbs	Fat

Snacks

Time	Items	Serving	Cals	Sugar	Protein	Fiber	Carbs	Fat

Total

Serving	Cals	Sugar	Protein	Fiber	Carbs	Fat

Date _____

Breakfast

Time	Items	Serving	Cals	Sugar	Protein	Fiber	Carbs	Fat

Lunch

Time	Items	Serving	Cals	Sugar	Protein	Fiber	Carbs	Fat

Dinner

Time	Items	Serving	Cals	Sugar	Protein	Fiber	Carbs	Fat

Snacks

Time	Items	Serving	Cals	Sugar	Protein	Fiber	Carbs	Fat

Total

Serving	Cals	Sugar	Protein	Fiber	Carbs	Fat

Date _____

Breakfast

Time	Items	Serving	Cals	Sugar	Protein	Fiber	Carbs	Fat

Lunch

Time	Items	Serving	Cals	Sugar	Protein	Fiber	Carbs	Fat

Dinner

Time	Items	Serving	Cals	Sugar	Protein	Fiber	Carbs	Fat

Snacks

Time	Items	Serving	Cals	Sugar	Protein	Fiber	Carbs	Fat

Total

Serving	Cals	Sugar	Protein	Fiber	Carbs	Fat

Date _____

Breakfast

Time	Items	Serving	Cals	Sugar	Protein	Fiber	Carbs	Fat

Lunch

Time	Items	Serving	Cals	Sugar	Protein	Fiber	Carbs	Fat

Dinner

Time	Items	Serving	Cals	Sugar	Protein	Fiber	Carbs	Fat

Snacks

Time	Items	Serving	Cals	Sugar	Protein	Fiber	Carbs	Fat

Total

Serving	Cals	Sugar	Protein	Fiber	Carbs	Fat

Date _____

Breakfast

Time	Items	Serving	Cals	Sugar	Protein	Fiber	Carbs	Fat

Lunch

Time	Items	Serving	Cals	Sugar	Protein	Fiber	Carbs	Fat

Dinner

Time	Items	Serving	Cals	Sugar	Protein	Fiber	Carbs	Fat

Snacks

Time	Items	Serving	Cals	Sugar	Protein	Fiber	Carbs	Fat

Total

Serving	Cals	Sugar	Protein	Fiber	Carbs	Fat

Date _____

Breakfast

Time	Items	Serving	Cals	Sugar	Protein	Fiber	Carbs	Fat

Lunch

Time	Items	Serving	Cals	Sugar	Protein	Fiber	Carbs	Fat

Dinner

Time	Items	Serving	Cals	Sugar	Protein	Fiber	Carbs	Fat

Snacks

Time	Items	Serving	Cals	Sugar	Protein	Fiber	Carbs	Fat

Total

Serving	Cals	Sugar	Protein	Fiber	Carbs	Fat

Date _____

Breakfast

Time	Items	Serving	Cals	Sugar	Protein	Fiber	Carbs	Fat

Lunch

Time	Items	Serving	Cals	Sugar	Protein	Fiber	Carbs	Fat

Dinner

Time	Items	Serving	Cals	Sugar	Protein	Fiber	Carbs	Fat

Snacks

Time	Items	Serving	Cals	Sugar	Protein	Fiber	Carbs	Fat

Total

Serving	Cals	Sugar	Protein	Fiber	Carbs	Fat

Date _____

Breakfast

Time	Items	Serving	Cals	Sugar	Protein	Fiber	Carbs	Fat

Lunch

Time	Items	Serving	Cals	Sugar	Protein	Fiber	Carbs	Fat

Dinner

Time	Items	Serving	Cals	Sugar	Protein	Fiber	Carbs	Fat

Snacks

Time	Items	Serving	Cals	Sugar	Protein	Fiber	Carbs	Fat

Total

Serving	Cals	Sugar	Protein	Fiber	Carbs	Fat

Date _____

Breakfast

Time	Items	Serving	Cals	Sugar	Protein	Fiber	Carbs	Fat

Lunch

Time	Items	Serving	Cals	Sugar	Protein	Fiber	Carbs	Fat

Dinner

Time	Items	Serving	Cals	Sugar	Protein	Fiber	Carbs	Fat

Snacks

Time	Items	Serving	Cals	Sugar	Protein	Fiber	Carbs	Fat

Total

Serving	Cals	Sugar	Protein	Fiber	Carbs	Fat

Date _____

Breakfast

Time	Items	Serving	Cals	Sugar	Protein	Fiber	Carbs	Fat

Lunch

Time	Items	Serving	Cals	Sugar	Protein	Fiber	Carbs	Fat

Dinner

Time	Items	Serving	Cals	Sugar	Protein	Fiber	Carbs	Fat

Snacks

Time	Items	Serving	Cals	Sugar	Protein	Fiber	Carbs	Fat

Total

Serving	Cals	Sugar	Protein	Fiber	Carbs	Fat

Date _____

Breakfast

Time	Items	Serving	Cals	Sugar	Protein	Fiber	Carbs	Fat

Lunch

Time	Items	Serving	Cals	Sugar	Protein	Fiber	Carbs	Fat

Dinner

Time	Items	Serving	Cals	Sugar	Protein	Fiber	Carbs	Fat

Snacks

Time	Items	Serving	Cals	Sugar	Protein	Fiber	Carbs	Fat

Total

Serving	Cals	Sugar	Protein	Fiber	Carbs	Fat

Date _____

Breakfast

Time	Items	Serving	Cals	Sugar	Protein	Fiber	Carbs	Fat

Lunch

Time	Items	Serving	Cals	Sugar	Protein	Fiber	Carbs	Fat

Dinner

Time	Items	Serving	Cals	Sugar	Protein	Fiber	Carbs	Fat

Snacks

Time	Items	Serving	Cals	Sugar	Protein	Fiber	Carbs	Fat

Total

Serving	Cals	Sugar	Protein	Fiber	Carbs	Fat

Date _____

Breakfast

Time	Items	Serving	Cals	Sugar	Protein	Fiber	Carbs	Fat

Lunch

Time	Items	Serving	Cals	Sugar	Protein	Fiber	Carbs	Fat

Dinner

Time	Items	Serving	Cals	Sugar	Protein	Fiber	Carbs	Fat

Snacks

Time	Items	Serving	Cals	Sugar	Protein	Fiber	Carbs	Fat

Total

Serving	Cals	Sugar	Protein	Fiber	Carbs	Fat

Date _____

Breakfast

Time	Items	Serving	Cals	Sugar	Protein	Fiber	Carbs	Fat

Lunch

Time	Items	Serving	Cals	Sugar	Protein	Fiber	Carbs	Fat

Dinner

Time	Items	Serving	Cals	Sugar	Protein	Fiber	Carbs	Fat

Snacks

Time	Items	Serving	Cals	Sugar	Protein	Fiber	Carbs	Fat

Total

Serving	Cals	Sugar	Protein	Fiber	Carbs	Fat

Date _____

Breakfast

Time	Items	Serving	Cals	Sugar	Protein	Fiber	Carbs	Fat

Lunch

Time	Items	Serving	Cals	Sugar	Protein	Fiber	Carbs	Fat

Dinner

Time	Items	Serving	Cals	Sugar	Protein	Fiber	Carbs	Fat

Snacks

Time	Items	Serving	Cals	Sugar	Protein	Fiber	Carbs	Fat

Total

Serving	Cals	Sugar	Protein	Fiber	Carbs	Fat

Date _____

Breakfast

Time	Items	Serving	Cals	Sugar	Protein	Fiber	Carbs	Fat

Lunch

Time	Items	Serving	Cals	Sugar	Protein	Fiber	Carbs	Fat

Dinner

Time	Items	Serving	Cals	Sugar	Protein	Fiber	Carbs	Fat

Snacks

Time	Items	Serving	Cals	Sugar	Protein	Fiber	Carbs	Fat

Total

Serving	Cals	Sugar	Protein	Fiber	Carbs	Fat

Thank you.

We hope you enjoyed our book.

As a small family company, your feedbeack is very important for us.

Please let us knou how you like our book at:

stromplklaus@yahoo.com

CPSIA information can be obtained
at www.ICGtesting.com
Printed in the USA
BVHW060033161121
621700BV00011B/335